PREDATOR VS PREY

HOW SHARKS AND OTHER FISH ATTACK

TIM HARRIS

PowerKiDS press

Published in 2026
by The Rosen Publishing Group, Inc.
2544 Clinton Street, Buffalo, NY 14224

First published in Great Britain in 2021 by Wayland

Editor: Amy Pimperton
Design: www.smartdesignstudio.co.uk
Picture research: Diana Morris

Cataloging-in-Publication Data

Names: Harris, Tim.

Title: How sharks and other fish attack / Tim Harris.

Description: Buffalo, NY : PowerKids Press, 2026. | Series: Predator vs. prey | Includes glossary and index.

Identifiers: ISBN 9781499454277 (pbk.) | ISBN 9781499454284 (library bound) | ISBN 9781499454291 (ebook)

Subjects: LCSH: Predatory aquatic animals--Juvenile literature. | Fishes--Behavior--Juvenile literature. | Sharks--Behavior--Juvenile literature. | Predation (Biology)--Juvenile literature.

Classification: LCC QL639.3 H377 2026 | DDC 597.153--dc23

Picture credits:

Nature PL: Franco Banfi 8b; Jane Burton 21t; David Shale 5br, 22, 31b; Solvin Zank 23t. Shutterstock: Aaronejbull87 2bl, 4bl; Alizada Studios 15t; Amplion 29bl; Apple Pho 19t; Silke Baron 12; Bearacreative 4br; Bigone 20; Bluehand 13t; BlueRingMedia 19cr; Eno Boy 21c; BugBoxx Production 25cl; Ramon Cattero front cover b, 1c, 4c; Coulanges 7t; Daulon 7cl, 11cl; De-frozen 25cr; Dive-hive 11t; Valerii Eviakhov 28; BW Folsom 7b; Frantisekhojdysz 10, 30t; Greens and Blues 1r, 3tl,13b, 27b; Guentermanaus 5c; HappyPictures 13cl, 23cl; Haveseen 2br, 18; Eric Isselee 9t; Andrea Izzotti 9b; Kletr 5bl; Vetra Kori 7cr; Tomas Kotouc 14; Kozh 13cr; MP Kullimratchai 16; Chatchai Kusolsinchai back cover r; Love Lego 11b; Maquiladora 15br; Gena Melendrez back cover c, 2bc, 29br; Roger Millan front cover tr; Kseniia Mnasina 21bl; Mophart Creation 21br; NataLima 23cr; Okliii 11cr; Oleg7799 17cr, 27cr; Wutttichook Panichwarapun 27t; Patrimonio designs ltd 27cl; Grigorii Pisotsckii 24; Janos Rautinen 15bl; Sail Far Dive Deep 3tc, 5t; Save Jungle 9cl, 15c; Olga Serova 29c; Natali Snailcat 19cl; Spread the design 9cr; Stubblefield Photography 1l, 23b; Dan Thornberg 26; Bodor Tivadar 17cl;Tmagalhaesrp 25t; Sergey Uryadnikov 6; VisionDive 3tr, 17b; Vojce 17t; Richard Whitcombe front cover tl; Krzysztof Winnik 29t; Tee Wong 19b; Danny Ye back cover l, 25b.

Manufactured in the United States of America

CPSIA Compliance Information: Batch #CSPK26. For further information contact Rosen Publishing at 1-800-237-9932.

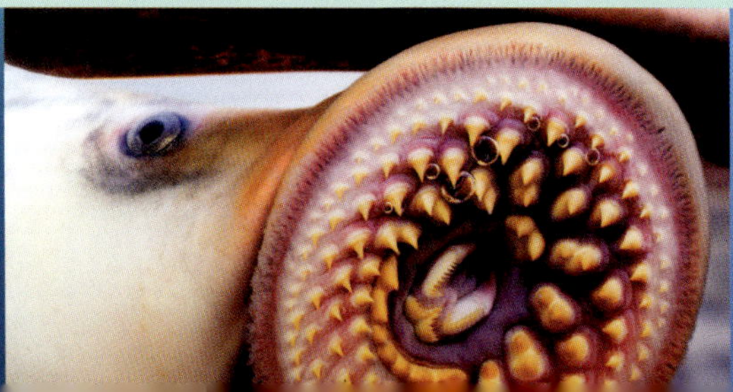

CONTENTS

FISH PREDATORS

Fish make up a diverse group of vertebrate animals. Some fish have bony skeletons, whereas others, such as sharks, have skeletons made of cartilage. Fish live in water and have gills – although not all fish breathe by absorbing oxygen from the water through their gills. The bodies of most fish are covered with protective scales and a layer of slippery mucus.

Some fish are predators. Sharks are one of the most well-known predatory fish and are feared as aggressive, razor-toothed killers. The iconic great white is probably the most feared of all. Fish vary in size, too. Whale sharks may reach 40 feet (12 m) long, whereas the infantfish may grow to only a half inch (1.2 cm) in length.

Vast numbers of fish species live in the ocean. They are perfectly adapted to this saltwater habitat and many will swim huge distances in a lifetime. Some, such as lionfish, live close to the shore in warmer waters, whereas deep-sea fish, such as anglerfish, inhabit the cold, dark depths.

GREAT WHITE SHARK

WHALE SHARK

LIONFISH

Not all fish live in the ocean. Aggressive piranhas live in South American rivers. Pike lurk in rivers and lakes, patiently waiting for prey to come within striking range. Salmon live in both saltwater and freshwater. As young, they migrate to the sea and then return to rivers to mate as adults.

PIRANHA

PIKE

ANGLERFISH

Fish are as varied as the methods they use to capture their prey. Some fish use power or speed to capture prey. Others use camouflage, electricity, or trickery to snare a meal. This book uncovers some of the incredible ways these fascinating animals survive and thrive – read on to find out more.

GREAT WHITE SHARK VS. BOTTLENOSE DOLPHIN: AMBUSH

Fearsome great white sharks are perfect ocean killers. These apex predators – and the world's largest predatory fish – live in all warm oceans. Fully-grown adults can reach 20 feet (6 m) in length. They hunt seals, sea lions, dolphins, other sharks, and even small whales, often ambushing them from below at great speed. Apart from people, great white sharks' only enemies are orcas (killer whales).

APEX PREDATOR: AN ANIMAL AT THE TOP OF A FOOD CHAIN

AN EXTRA SENSE

As well as excellent sight, hearing, touch, smell, and taste, a shark has a sixth sense. It can detect electricity and magnetism with sensors in the snout called ampullae of Lorenzini. With this sixth sense, a shark can navigate and detect prey in the water. A great white shark can sense the movement of an animal up to 820 feet (250 m) away.

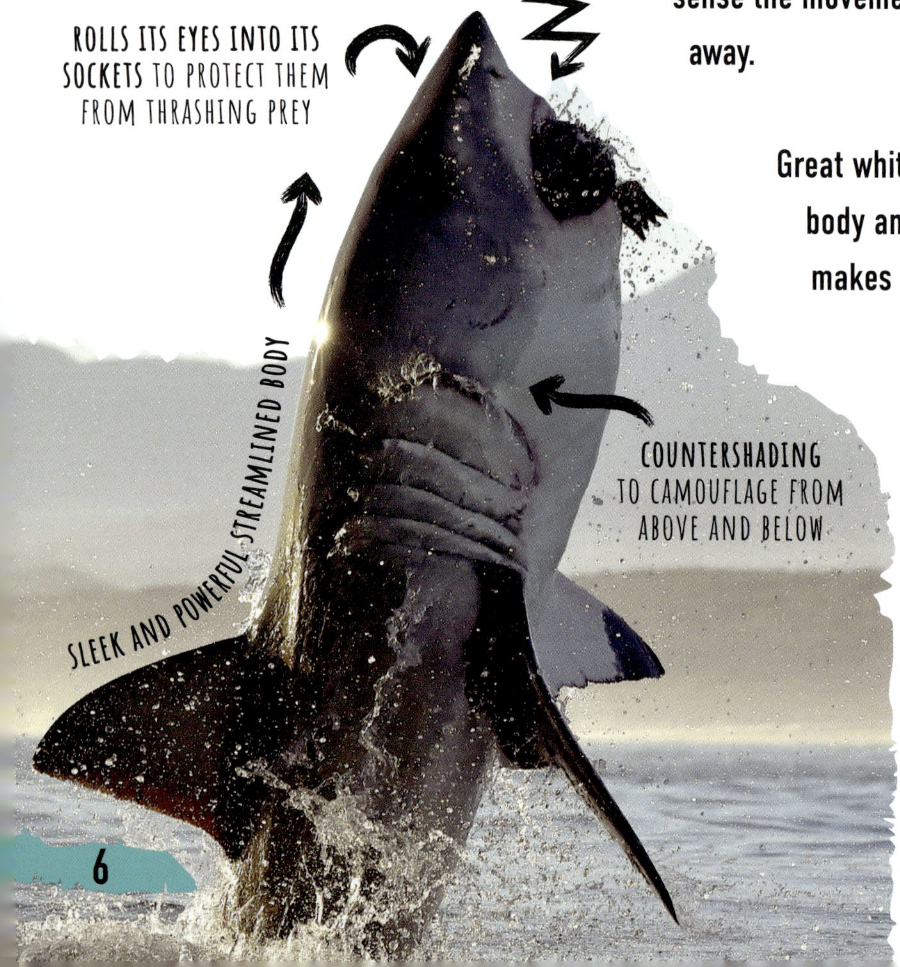

Great white sharks have a dark-colored upper body and a pale belly. This countershading makes it difficult for prey animals to spot the shark either from above or from below. Powering up from the deep, great white sharks sometimes smash into or grab prey at the water's surface.

AMPULLAE OF LORENZINI WORK PARTICULARLY WELL UNDERWATER BECAUSE ELECTRICAL CURRENTS TRAVEL MORE EASILY IN WATER THAN IN AIR.

AMBUSH: TO LIE IN WAIT AND THEN LAUNCH A SURPRISE ATTACK

BOTTLENOSE DOLPHIN

Dolphins are intelligent, fish-eating aquatic mammals called cetaceans. Excellent swimmers and divers, bottlenose dolphins can leap 20 feet (6 m) out of the ocean. Dolphins track the shoals of fish they eat using echolocation. This works by making rapid clicking noises and listening for the echoes. In this way, the dolphins can tell how far away the fish are and the direction they are swimming. They also use echolocation to detect predators, such as great white sharks.

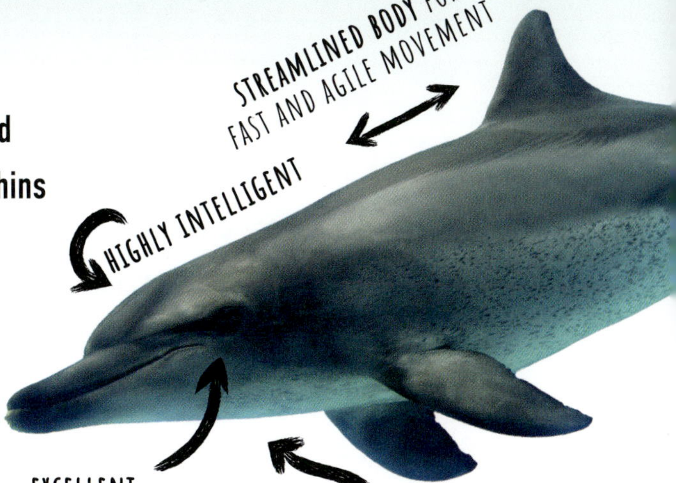

GREAT WHITE SHARK STATS

Length: up to 20 ft (6 m)
Weight: up to 5,070 lb (2,300 kg)
Max speed: 30 mph (48 kph)

Six amazing senses; very fast swimmer; 300 sharp, serrated teeth; powerful jaws

VS.

BOTTLENOSE DOLPHIN STATS

Length: 13 ft (4 m)
Weight: 660 lb (300 kg)
Max speed: 12 mph (20 kph)

Highly intelligent; fast swimmer; excellent eyesight; uses echolocation for attack and defense

A GREAT WHITE SHARK'S SERRATED TEETH HELP IT TO TEAR THROUGH FLESH.

SHAKE IT OFF!

With 300 or so deadly, serrated teeth clamped around an unlucky victim, the shark shakes its head from side to side to saw off chunks of flesh. Sometimes it bites prey hard so that it draws blood, then waits for the victim to bleed to death.

BULL SHARK vs. HIPPOPOTAMUS: BUMP-AND-BITE

Bull sharks are blunt-nosed, sharp-toothed killers. They are unusual among shark species because they are equally at home hunting in salty coastal waters or warm freshwater rivers. These fish may venture far up large rivers, such as the Amazon or Mississippi. Bull sharks will attack and eat pretty much any animal they come across. Mostly, they kill fish, squid, and turtles, but in rivers they sometimes encounter other animals, including rats, dogs, antelope, and even hippos!

STRATEGY: A PLAN OF ACTION

MURKY LURKERS

Although bull sharks don't have great vision, like other sharks, they have a fantastic sense of smell. This means they can sniff out their prey in the murky water of muddy rivers, where their prey can't see them approach. A bull shark has an unusual attack strategy: when it gets close to prey, it head-butts it hard. This may confuse, stun, or even kill its victim, allowing the shark to bite into it with its razor-sharp teeth.
This is called a bump-and-bite attack.

BULL SHARKS CAN SURVIVE IN FRESHWATER HABITATS FOR LONG PERIODS OF TIME.

BUMP-AND-BITE: TO DELIBERATELY BUMP INTO THE VICTIM BEFORE BITING

HIPPOPOTAMUS

Hippos are massive and highly dangerous mammals that spend a lot of time in African rivers and estuaries. They use their long, sharp canine teeth for attack and defense. Bull sharks have been known to bump-and-bite hippos, but a hippo's tough skin and aggressive nature mean that a bull shark would struggle to kill a fully-grown adult. A baby hippo is an easier target – if the bull shark can get past the baby's mother!

BULL SHARK STATS

Length: 7-11 ft (2.1-3.4 m)
Weight: up to 1,120 lb (508 kg)
Max speed: 10 mph (16 kph)

Great sense of smell allows it to hunt in murky water; stuns prey with head-butt; attacks at speed; very aggressive

VS.

HIPPOPOTAMUS STATS

Length: 11 ft (3.4 m) (males are longer)
Weight: 7,050 lb (3,200 kg) (males are heavier)
Max speed: 20 mph (32 kph) on land

Strong bite; long canine teeth; very aggressive; can hold its breath underwater for around 5 minutes

HUMAN ENCOUNTERS

Bull sharks are considered one of the most dangerous shark species to humans. There is a risk of bull sharks coming into contact with unsuspecting people enjoying a dip or a paddle in the warm, shallow waters off the coast ...

TIGER SHARK vs. GREEN TURTLE: SCENT

Deadly tiger sharks are nighttime predators and real loners. When hungry, they will attack any creature they come across. Their victims include fish, seals, and dolphins. Tiger sharks' teeth are so sharp they can slice through flesh, bone, and even the shells of green sea turtles, which are a particular favorite. In their determination to get a meal, they sometimes crush and swallow things that aren't alive – including license plates, tires, and baseballs!

SUPER SNIFFERS

Tiger sharks' superb senses help them find their prey and – like other sharks – they can detect the electricity given off by other animals. They can also pick up and track the faint scent of distant prey and the blood of injured animals. A tiger shark can smell one part of blood in one million parts of water – the equivalent of a teaspoon of blood in a small swimming pool. A green sea turtle makes a slow-moving target for this fast fish.

LONER: ANIMAL THAT USUALLY PREFERS TO LIVE AND HUNT ALONE

SCENT: THE DISTINCTIVE SMELL OF AN ANIMAL

GREEN SEA TURTLE

The green sea turtle is a large species of sea turtle. Its tough, smooth shell (also called a carapace) offers this slow-moving reptile some protection from predators, but a hungry tiger shark will have no problem slicing a turtle open. Sometimes a turtle's only chance to escape a predator is to dive down and stay there, as they can hold their breath for up to 7 hours.

TIGER SHARK STATS

Length: up to 15 ft (4.5 m)
Weight: up to 1,980 lb (900 kg)
Max speed: 20 mph (32 kph)

Superb senses; fast attack; strong jaws; sharp teeth that are adapted to slice through turtle shells

VS.

GREEN SEA TURTLE STATS

Length: up to 4 ft (1.2 m)
Weight: 770 lb (350 kg)
Max speed: 2 mph (3 kph)

Hard shell offers some protection; swims close to shores and in shallow waters; can dive and hold its breath for up to 7 hours

FEATHERY SNACKS

Off the coast of Hawaii, tiger sharks are known to catch and eat young albatrosses. Adults birds are strong fliers, but juveniles often plop down into the water on leaving their nest. Scavenging tiger sharks wait to gobble up the unwitting seabirds.

MORAY EEL vs. LIONFISH: TWO SETS OF JAWS

Giant moray eels, venomous lionfish, and coral groupers are three kinds of fish that live around coral reefs in the warm waters of the Indian Ocean. Hiding away in crevices during the day, moray eels usually go hunting when it gets dark. These big, aggressive fish don't like to be disturbed and sometimes even attack human divers who come too close to their lair. Like all eels, they are long and thin, which means they can swim into holes in search of prey.

VENOMOUS BARBS? NO PROBLEM!

When an eel grabs prey with its teeth, a second set of jaws in the back of the throat move forward and backward to grip and then pull the prey down the eel's long throat. Marine scientists have spotted how moray eels deal with a lionfish's venom-tipped spines. The eel coils around the lionfish and then flips it with its jaws to eat the lionfish head-first. This causes the spines to fold down, making it less likely to sting the eel's throat as it slips down.

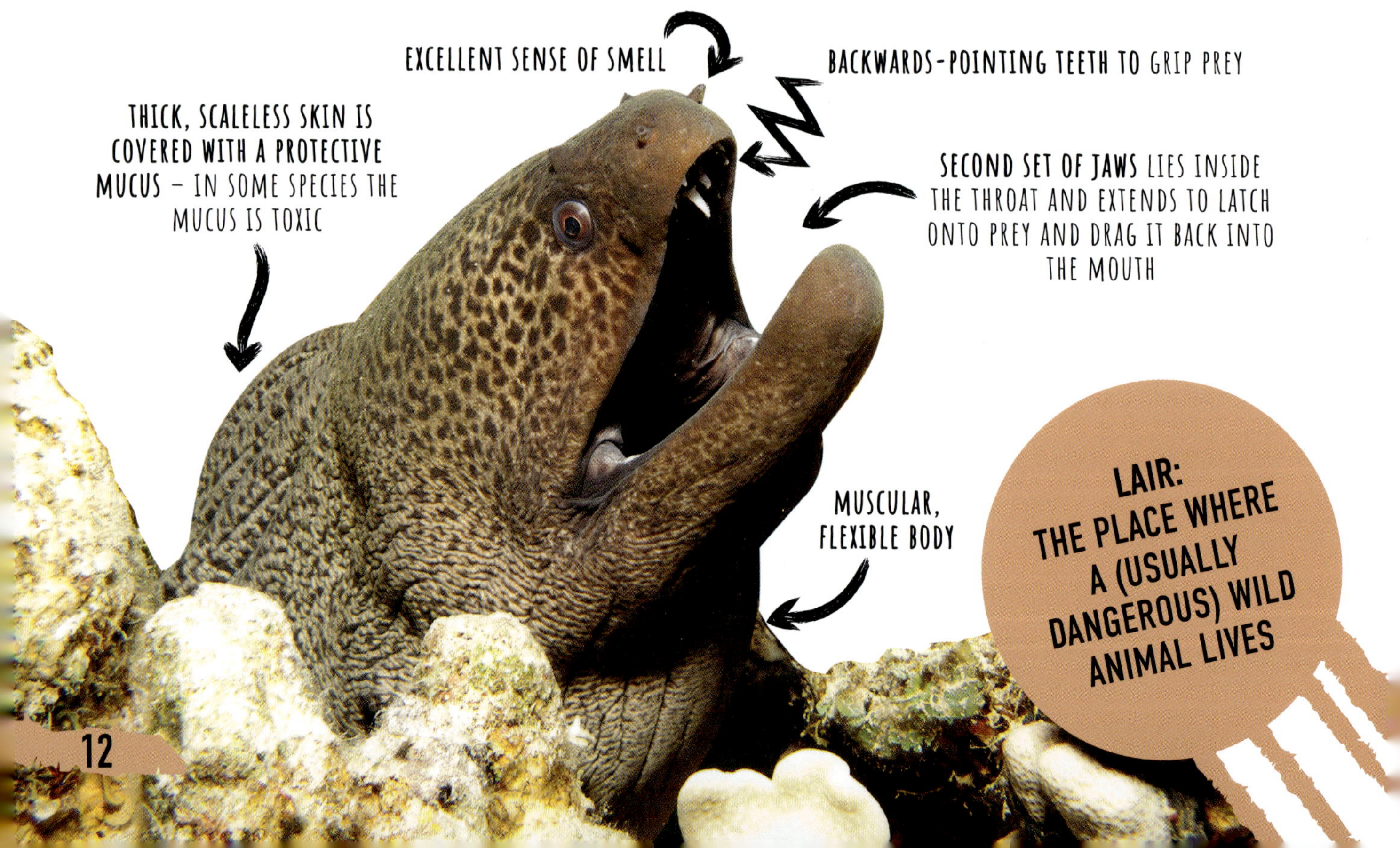

LAIR: THE PLACE WHERE A (USUALLY DANGEROUS) WILD ANIMAL LIVES

LIONFISH

Lionfish are incredible-looking creatures with 18 long spines. They may be beautiful, but these fish have become an invasive species in some parts of the world. Lionfish have few enemies because their bright stripes warn would-be predators that their spines carry deadly poison. The giant moray eel is one fish that does eat them, however.

GIANT MORAY EEL STATS

Length: 10 ft (3 m)
Weight: 65 lb (30 kg)

Strong jaws, sharp teeth; thin enough to access narrow cracks and crevices; flexible body for handling prey; excellent sense of smell

VS.

LIONFISH STATS

Length: 14 in (35.5 cm)
Weight: 1 lb (0.4 kg)

Venomous spines; invasive species with few natural predators; fast reflexes; they sometimes spread their fins out to herd smaller fish

TEAMWORK

Coral groupers sometimes team up with moray eels to catch prey hiding in a hole in the reef that is too small for the grouper to enter. It will swim to an eel's lair and signal to it by shaking its head. If the eel is hungry, it goes into the hole, catches the fish, and also scares out any other fish – which the grouper gobbles up!

CORAL GROUPER

HAMMERHEAD SHARK VS. SHORT-TAIL STINGRAY: ELECTROMAGNETISM

As its name suggests, a hammerhead shark has a head shaped like a hammer, with one eye on each side. Its mouth is full of sharp, serrated teeth. Like other sharks, it has the sixth sense to detect electromagnetic charges in water. The underside of the head is packed with these electroreceptors – called ampullae of Lorenzini (see page 6). Since its head is so wide, a hammerhead is better at sensing the presence of prey than other sharks. It can even figure out if a stingray is buried in the sand.

PINNED DOWN

A hammerhead swims close to the seabed, using its eyes and electrical sensors to search for prey. It swings its head back and forth, scanning the sand. If it locates a stingray, it uses the side of its head to pin its prey to the seabed and bites chunks out of the ray's wings. Because it is held down, the stingray finds it hard to use its stinging tail to fight back.

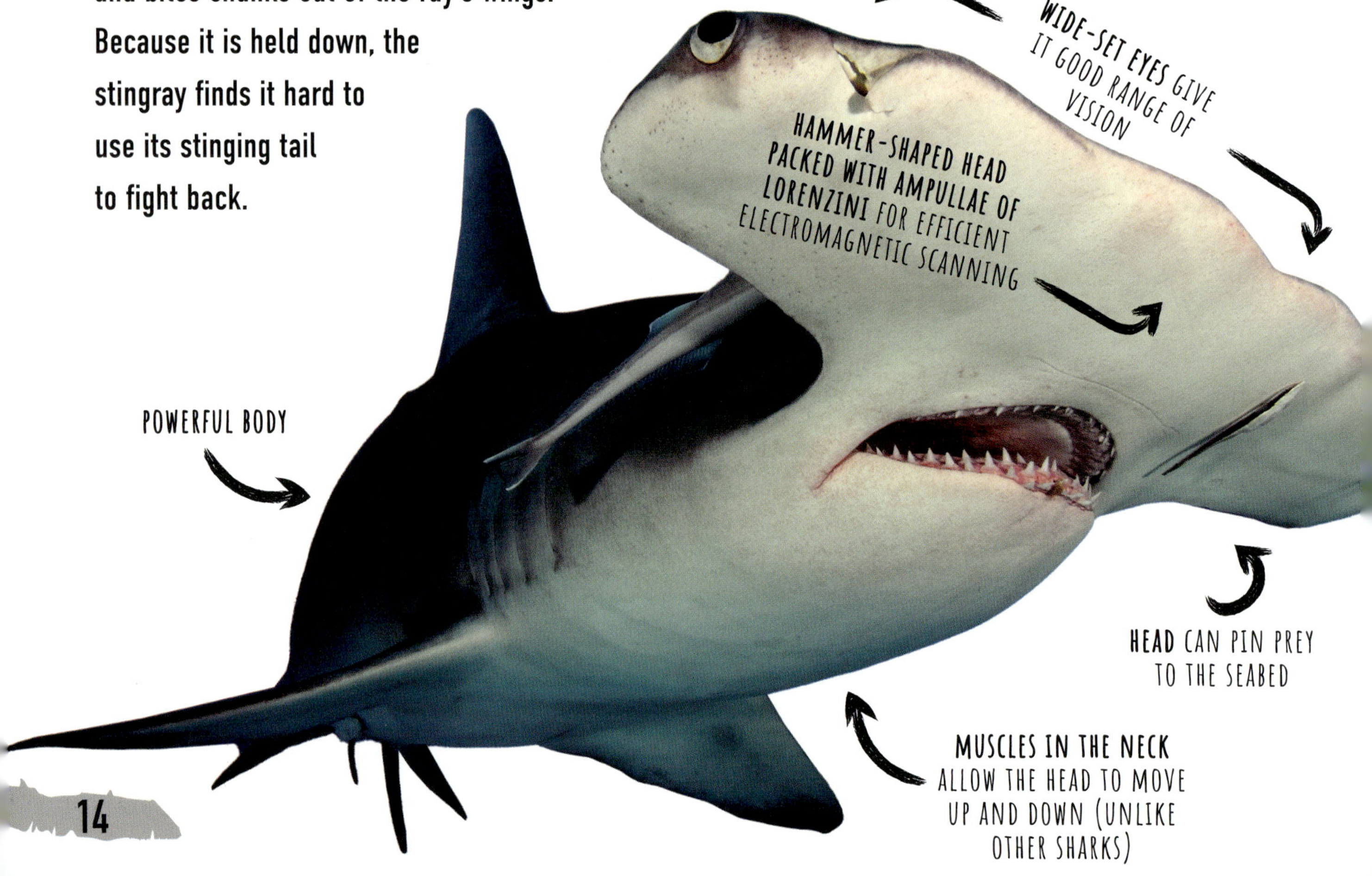

ELECTROMAGNETISM: THE FORCE CREATED BY ELECTRICITY AND MAGNETISM

SHORT-TAIL STINGRAY

Stingrays are large fish that live close to the seabed, where they feed on fish, worms, and crustaceans. They have a flattened body, broad diamond-shaped pectoral fins, or "wings," and a long, thin tail. They have one or two saw-edged spines, or barbs, on their tail. These contain deadly venom, powerful enough to kill most animals.

FLAT BODY TO HIDE UNDER THE SEABED

STINGRAYS ALSO HAVE AMPULLAE OF LORENZINI TO DETECT PREDATORS AND PREY.

DEADLY BARBS ON THE END OF THE TAIL

If there is danger, the stingray has two means of defense. During the day, it buries itself under the sand on the seabed and hopes that predators don't see it. When threatened, a stingray holds its tail over its back like a scorpion and then tries to stab the barbs into its attacker.

VENOM: POISON OR TOXINS PRODUCED BY SOME ANIMALS

UNLIKE MANY OTHER SHARKS, SOME SPECIES OF HAMMERHEAD SWIM IN LARGE GROUPS OR SCHOOLS.

HAMMERHEAD SHARK STATS

Length: up to 20 ft (6 m)
Weight: up to 1,000 lb (454 kg)
Max speed: 25 mph (40 kph)

Hammer-shaped head; sharp teeth; highly tuned electromagnetic sensors

VS.

SHORT-TAIL STINGRAY STATS

Length: 13 ft (4 m)
Weight: 770 lb (350 kg)
Max speed: unknown

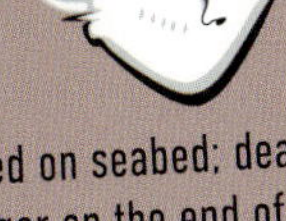

Camouflaged on seabed; deadly venomous stinger on the end of its tail

REEF STONEFISH VS. GOBY: SPEED

It's not big and it's not strong, but the reef stonefish is one of the deadliest fish in the ocean. There are two reasons for this: when it attacks, it does so faster than the blink of an eye; and it has the most lethal poison of any fish. This fish lives in coral reefs in the tropical waters of the Indian and Pacific Oceans.

PERFECT CAMOUFLAGE

Lying in wait and half buried on the seabed, a stonefish looks like a lump of coral. It has rough skin and may be brown or gray, with patches of red, orange, or yellow. This makes the perfect camouflage to fool any fish or shrimp that happens to swim past.

It takes 0.1 seconds for you to blink your eye, but that's five times as long as it takes a stonefish to suck in and swallow prey. A stonefish attack is too fast for the human eye to see. It has to be filmed with a high-speed camera, then played in slow motion. If threatened by a larger fish, a reef stonefish will attack with its 13 venomous spines. They carry enough venom to kill many animals.

YELLOW CLOWN GOBY

This pretty little fish lives among coral reefs, sheltering from predators among the branches of tropical corals and defending its territory. But this fish has a trick of its own! It is covered with a poisonous and bitter mucus to deter some predators. These interesting animals can also change sex. They are all born female, but some will change to male if the need arises – and can then change back to female!

HIDES AMONG CORAL FOR PROTECTION

REEF STONEFISH STATS

Length: 16 in (40 cm)
Weight: 4 lb (2 kg)
Max speed: usually stationary

Lightning-fast reactions; camouflage, deadly venom

VS.

YELLOW CLOWN GOBY STATS

Width: 1 in (2.5 cm)
Weight: less than an ounce
Max speed: unknown, but slow

Covered in toxic mucus; actively defends its territory; can change sex

CAMOUFLAGE: FUR OR SKIN MARKINGS TO HIDE AN ANIMAL IN ITS HABITAT

WATCH YOUR STEP

When humans and stonefish come into contact, the result can be deadly. People wading in tropical waters have to watch where they tread, as stepping on one of these camouflaged animals is incredibly painful – and can be fatal.

MANTA RAY VS. KRILL: HERDING

Manta rays are oceanic giants, yet most of their prey is tiny. These tropical fish have a pair of massive, triangular pectoral fins on either side of their body and a long, thin tail. A fully grown manta ray may be 23 feet (7 m) across. It beats its fins slowly to drive itself through the water.

FILTER FEEDING

A manta ray has two smaller fins, called cephalic lobes, which it curls into an O shape to funnel water into its mouth. In this water is the ray's prey – krill and small fish. The water passes through the ray's mouth and out of slits called gill rakers that trap the prey. This kind of feeding is called filter feeding.

If a manta ray finds a big group of krill, it swims around them. It twists and turns and performs underwater somersaults to herd them together. When the krill are packed tightly, the ray swims quickly through them, sucking them up like a gigantic vacuum cleaner. Rays may feed alone or join groups of up to 50.

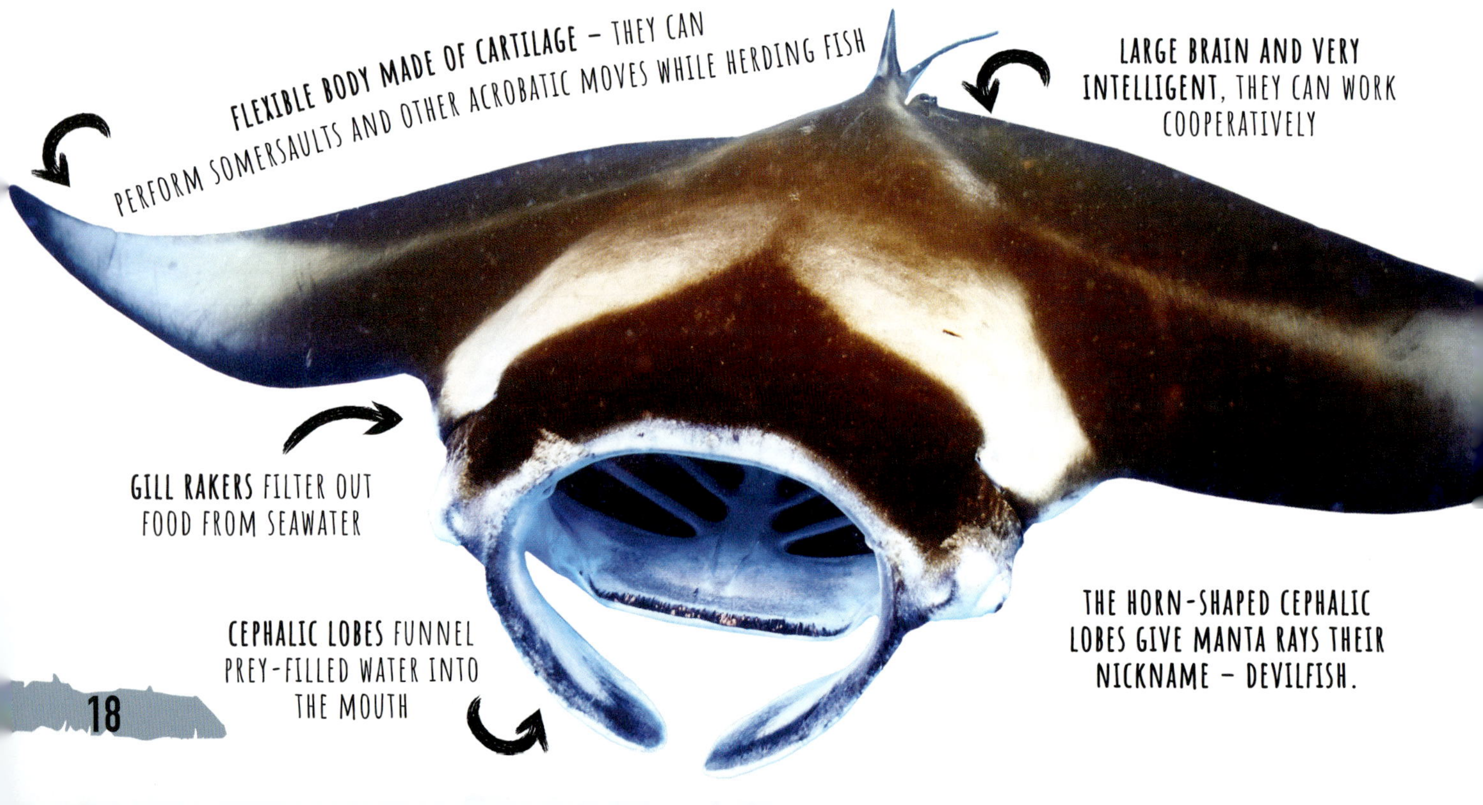

HERDING: TO MOVE A GROUP OF ANIMALS SO THEY ARE TIGHTLY PACKED TOGETHER

SOME SAFETY IN NUMBERS

KRILL

Most krill are only about 2 inches (5 cm) long, though some are larger. There are billions of them in the world's oceans and they are one of the animals at the bottom of the ocean food chain. Many other sea creatures depend on them for their food. Safety in numbers may help these small, defenseless animals to survive, but a hungry ray can eat many krill in one meal.

PECTORAL: RELATING TO THE CHEST OR BREAST

GIANT OCEANIC MANTA RAY STATS

Width: 23 ft (7 m)
Weight: usually around 3,000 lb (1,360 kg); some weigh over 4,400 lb (2,000 kg)
Max speed: 15 mph (24 kph)

Very large mouth; highly intelligent; flexible body

VS.

KRILL STATS

Length: up to 6 in (15 cm), but most species are around 2 in (5 cm) long
Weight: a few grams
Max speed: Unknown, but very slow

Defenseless, but swarms to find some safety in numbers

A WHALE SHARK DISPLAYS ITS DISTINCTIVE WIDE MOUTH.

OCEAN GIANTS

Several other ocean giants are filter feeders, including the magnificent whale shark, which is also the world's largest fish. Like the manta ray, it sucks in vast amounts of seawater and then filters the water out through its gills, trapping krill and other small marine animals.

ELECTRIC EEL

VS. BLACK GHOST KNIFEFISH: ELECTRIC SHOCK

There's a fish that lives in muddy, slow-moving rivers in South America that can defend itself and kill its prey with electric shocks. That fish is the electric eel, which has a snakelike body and gray or brown skin. It can swim forward or backward as it goes in search of a meal. Electric eels are not a true eels, but members of the knifefish family.

WEAK AND STRONG CURRENTS

Organs inside an electric eel's body make electricity. An eel sends out weak currents of electricity to communicate with other eels. If the water level in a river gets low, these fish are sometimes attacked by larger animals. If this happens, an eel can force its enemy to back off by leaping out of the water and delivering a massive electric shock.

Electric eels have sensory organs that detect the movements of prey animals in murky water where it's difficult to see anything. If a hungry eel comes across a fish, frog, or swimming rat, it moves in for the kill and sends out a devastating blast of 800 volts of electricity. This paralyzes the prey animal and the eel eats it.

ELECTRIC SHOCK: A SUDDEN JOLT OF ENERGY THROUGH THE BODY

BLACK GHOST KNIFEFISH

Among the many creatures that electric eels hunt are smaller members of its own knifefish family. The black ghost knifefish is a nocturnal hunter, feeding on even smaller fish and worms. Like the electric eel, it can also create an electric shock – but nowhere near as strong as that of an electric eel.

PARALYZE: TO CAUSE A BODY (OR BODY PART) TO BE UNABLE TO MOVE

ELECTRIC EEL STATS

Length: 6 ft (2 m)
Weight: 44 lb (20 kg)
Max speed: unknown, but it is fast

Senses other animals by the electric currents they produce; paralyzes prey with massive electric shocks; can swim forward and backward

VS.

BLACK GHOST KNIFEFISH STATS

Length: 20 in (50 cm)
Max speed: 0.25 mph (0.4 kph)

Hides during the day, but is active at night; can produce a weak electric current to communicate or to detect predators

DON'T MOVE A MUSCLE!

Electric eels sometimes use a weaker electric shock to force the muscles of their prey to twitch. This helps the eel pinpoint the victim, before darting in for the kill.

ANGLERFISH VS. SQUID: LURE

Anglerfish are some of the strangest creatures swimming in the ocean. They live far below the surface, where very little sunlight reaches. The fish take advantage of the darkness when they hunt. Football fish are type of anglerfish. The females are much larger than the males and they are almost spherical. One of their spines (called an illicium) hangs over the front of the fish. On the end of this spine is a blob, or esca, filled with bacteria that glow in the dark!

FISHING LURE

A female football fish floats almost motionless in the ocean depths, and its esca acts as a fishing lure. Other sea creatures – including fish, squid, and shrimp – come to investigate the light glowing in the darkness. If they swim close enough, the football fish sucks them into its huge mouth. Since its sharp teeth slant backward, anything drawn into the mouth can't escape. These fish can stretch themselves to make room for prey that is bigger than they are, up to 3 feet (1 m) long.

BACTERIA: SINGLE-CELLED ORGANISMS

LURE: TO TEMPT AN ANIMAL; BAIT ON THE END OF A HOOK OR LINE

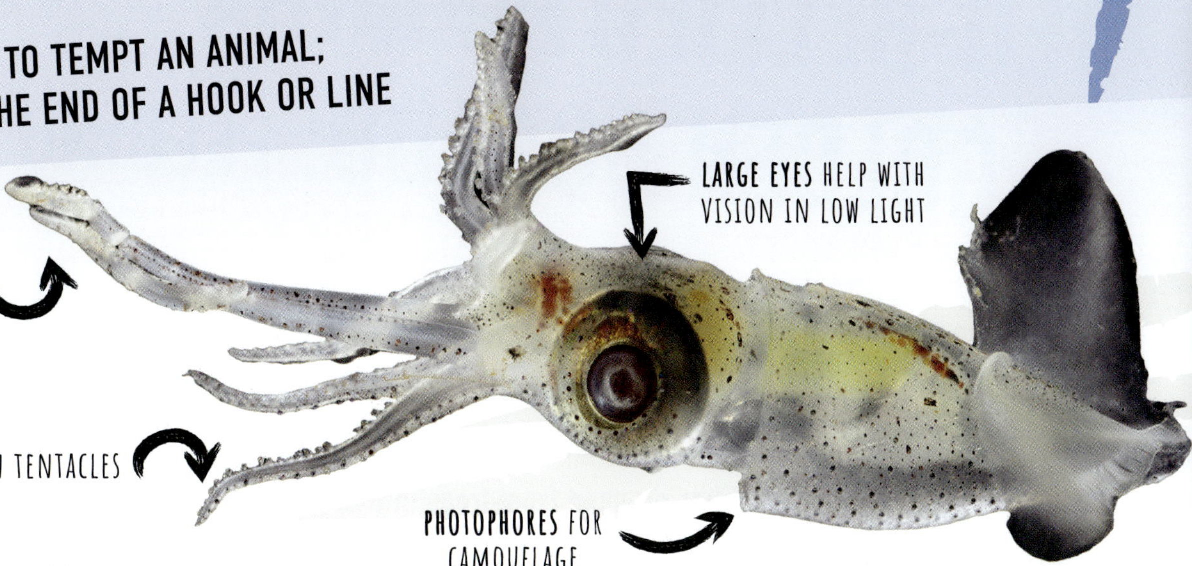

MIDWATER SQUID

The small midwater squid spends the day hiding in the murky ocean depths, up to 2,625 feet (800 m) below the surface. It has special organs on its underside called photophores that give off light. This is a defense against predators hunting in the water beneath – the lights help conceal it against the lighter water above. These squid eat tiny ocean invertebrates and may mistake an anglerfish's lure for a tasty snack – with deadly consequences!

ATLANTIC FOOTBALL FISH STATS

Length: 24 in (61 cm) (females); 1.5 in (4 cm) (males)
Weight: 25 lb (11 kg) (females); less than an ounce (males)
Max speed: sedentary

Tricks prey with its light lure; large mouth and sharp teeth; can expand its body to fit large prey

VS.

MIDWATER SQUID STATS

Width: 2 in (5 cm)
Weight: less than an ounce
Max speed: slow

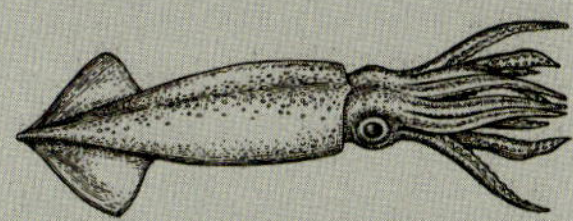

Camouflage; suckers and hooks on its tentacles; hides in dark ocean depths during the day

LONGLURE FROGFISH

FROGFISH

Frogfish are another type of anglerfish. These unusual fish are found on the ocean floor in tropical waters, often hiding among coral. They use a lure disguised as a worm to attract prey and then snatch it in the blink of an eye!

RED-BELLIED PIRANHA vs. GOLDEN DORADO: FEEDING FRENZY

Red-bellied piranhas have a reputation as ferocious predators. In fact, in the Brazilian Tupi language, *piranha* means "tooth fish." It is true that these South American river fish do have very sharp teeth, but they're rarely as dangerous as they are sometimes made out to be. Piranhas often eat fruit that has dropped from trees into their slow-moving rivers and they scavenge on dead animals that they find floating in the water. If there is nothing else to eat, piranhas may eat one another. This is called cannibalism.

MIND YOUR FINGERS!

It is not a good idea to stick your finger in a piranha's mouth, though. This fish has very strong jaw muscles and a powerful bite that clamps shut two sets of razor-sharp triangular teeth. But much of a piranha's diet is made up of fins nipped from the tails of larger fish.

If a shoal of piranhas come across a fish that is injured, a feeding frenzy may take place. The piranhas swarm around the helpless victim, tearing off chunks of flesh bite by bite. A shoal of frenzied piranhas is capable of stripping the flesh off a large predatory fish, such as a dorado, in minutes.

FEEDING FRENZY: WHEN A SHOAL OF FISH ALL TAKE BITES OUT OF THE SAME PREY ANIMAL

GOLDEN DORADO

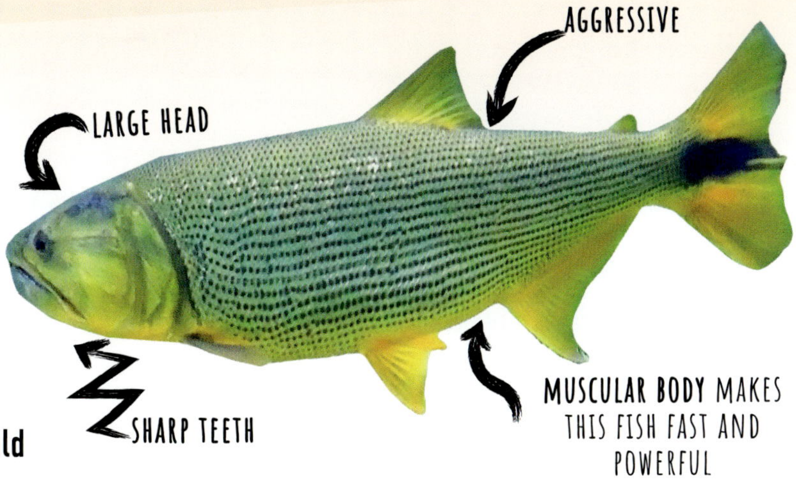

Also called the river tiger, the golden dorado is an apex predator patrolling the waters of South American rivers. They are very powerful and fast, and feed exclusively on other fish. A piranha would make a tasty snack. However, an injured dorado is no match for a shoal of piranhas that sense an opportunity for an easy meal ...

CANNIBAL: AN ANIMAL THAT EATS ANOTHER OF THE SAME SPECIES

RED-BELLIED PIRANHA STATS

Length: 14 in (35.5 cm)
Weight: 9 lb (4 kg)
Max speed: 15 mph (24 kph)

Sharp teeth and powerful bite; fast swimmer; aggressive; good sense of hearing

VS.

GOLDEN DORADO STATS

Length: up to 4 ft (1.2 m) (females are larger)
Weight: 40 lb (18 kg) (females are heavier)
Max speed: unknown, but can produce very fast bursts of speed

Aggressive and powerful; fast; sharp teeth

GOLIATH TIGERFISH

Piranhas and dorados are both a type of fish called a characin. Even scarier than the piranha or the dorado is another characin called the goliath tigerfish. Growing to lengths of around 5 feet (1.5 m), this monster hunts in the waters of the Congo River Basin in Africa. It has been known to attack humans and will eat baby Nile crocodiles!

SHEEPSHEAD FISH vs. FIDDLER CRAB: CRUSHING TEETH

A fish called the sheepshead lives in coastal waters on the Atlantic coast of North and South America. These fish have a greenish-silver body with five or six blackish vertical bars. The stripes give them their alternative name of "convict fish." The thing that makes sheepsheads really unusual, though, is their teeth.

A TOUGH DIET

Unlike most fish, sheepsheads have sharp, chisel-shaped front teeth (incisors), and strong, stubby back teeth (like human molars). There are three rows of these in the top jaw and two rows in the bottom jaw.

CONVICT: SOMEONE WHO IS IN PRISON FOR BREAKING THE LAW

These crushing and grinding teeth are a clue as to the sheepshead's diet. Sheepsheads specialize in eating crabs, oysters, clams, and barnacles. All of these animals have tough outer shells, which the fish break open with their amazing teeth. They scrape barnacles off rocks with their front teeth, then crush them with their back teeth to get at the soft flesh inside.

BACK TEETH FOR CRUSHING AND GRINDING HARD SHELLS

FRONT TEETH FOR SCRAPING PREY OFF ROCKS

STRONG JAW MUSCLES HELP TO CRUSH PREY

FIDDLER CRAB

Fiddler crabs are one of the sheepshead's favorite meals. Like all crabs, they have four pairs of legs and a single pair of grabbing claws. A thick, tough outer skeleton (exoskeleton) protects their soft insides. These crabs dig protective burrows in sand or mud, but they have to come out to feed and find mates.

SHEEPSHEAD FISH STATS

Length: up to 30 in (76 cm)
Weight: 22 lb (10 kg)
Max speed: slow

Highly adapted teeth for crushing shells

VS.

FIDDLER CRAB STATS

Width: up to 3 in (7.6 cm)
Weight: less than an ounce
Max speed: slow

Tough outer skeleton; hides in a burrow when not feeding

TOOTHY TRIGGERFISH

Colorful triggerfish have a similar mouthful of crushing teeth. Like sheepshead fish, triggerfish eat crustaceans, crushing and grinding the shells of their victims with their specially adapted teeth.

TITAN TRIGGERFISH

SEA LAMPREY vs. LAKE STURGEON: BLOODSUCKING

Sea lampreys are the bloodsuckers of the fish world. Despite their name, these long, thin fish do not spend the whole of their life at sea. Adults do live in saltwater, but they swim up rivers to mate and lay their eggs in freshwater. The young lampreys that hatch from the eggs live and grow in lakes and rivers for several years before swimming to the ocean.

MATE:
WHEN A MALE AND FEMALE OF THE SAME SPECIES ACT TO PRODUCE YOUNG

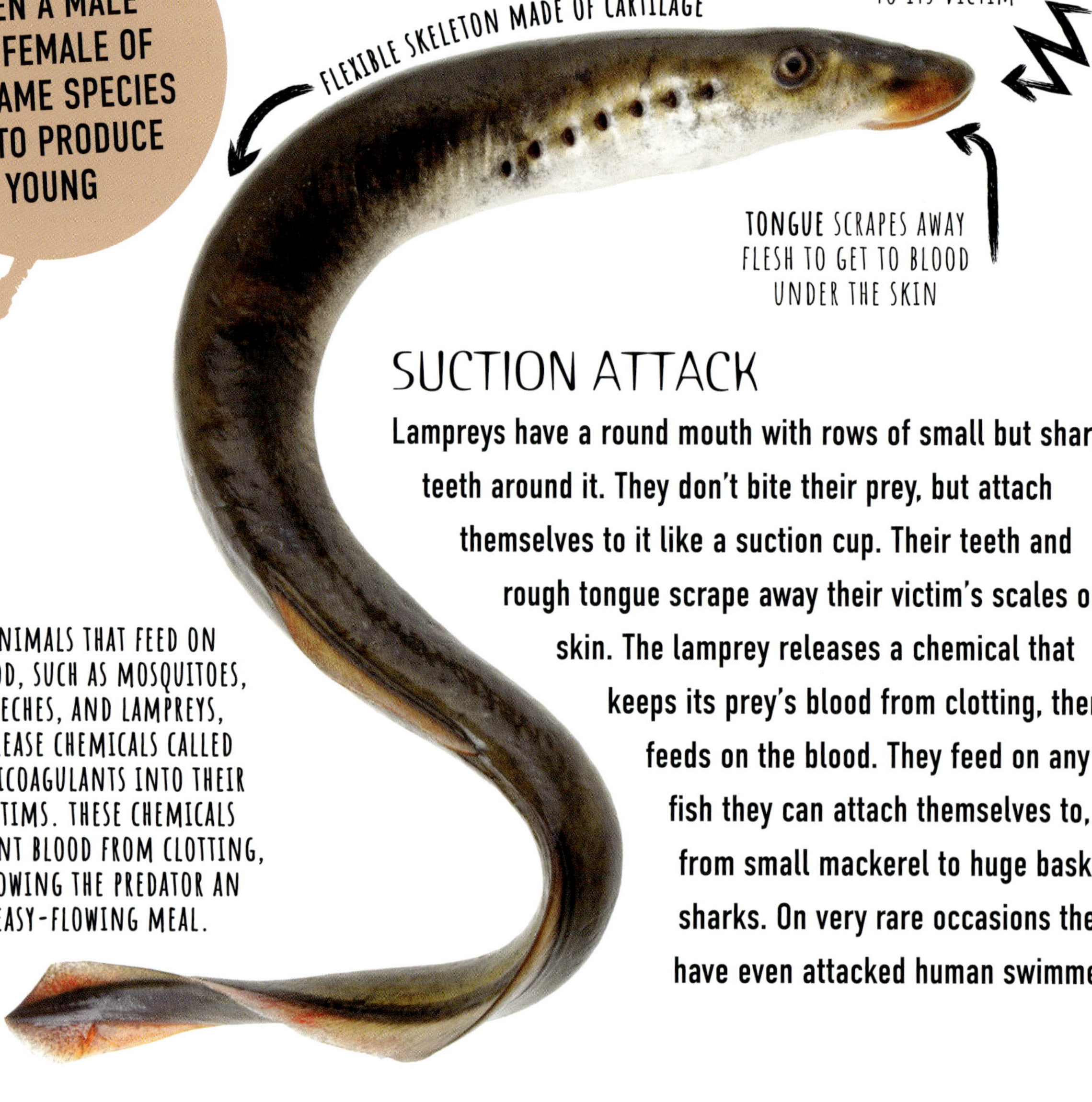

SUCTION ATTACK

Lampreys have a round mouth with rows of small but sharp teeth around it. They don't bite their prey, but attach themselves to it like a suction cup. Their teeth and rough tongue scrape away their victim's scales or skin. The lamprey releases a chemical that keeps its prey's blood from clotting, then feeds on the blood. They feed on any fish they can attach themselves to, from small mackerel to huge basking sharks. On very rare occasions they have even attacked human swimmers.

ANIMALS THAT FEED ON BLOOD, SUCH AS MOSQUITOES, LEECHES, AND LAMPREYS, RELEASE CHEMICALS CALLED ANTICOAGULANTS INTO THEIR VICTIMS. THESE CHEMICALS PREVENT BLOOD FROM CLOTTING, ALLOWING THE PREDATOR AN EASY-FLOWING MEAL.

BLOOD-SUCKING: FEEDING ON BLOOD FROM A LIVE VICTIM

LAKE STURGEON

In the Great Lakes of the United States and Canada, lamprey may attack fish such as sturgeon. The sturgeon search for clams and invertebrates on the bottoms of lakes. Sensory organs called barbels help it detect prey. Although they grow very much bigger than lampreys, there is little they can do if attacked. Despite their size, a sturgeon may not survive a lamprey attack – either bleeding to death or dying from an infection in the wound.

SEA LAMPREY STATS

Length: 4 ft (1.2 m)
Weight: 5 lb (2.3 kg)
Max speed: slow

Sharp teeth attach to prey; rough tongue scrapes away skin; releases chemical that keeps prey bleeding

VS.

LAKE STURGEON STATS

Width: 7 ft (2.1 m)
Weight: 240 lb (109 kg)
Max speed: slow

Large size, but slow

A LAMPREY DISPLAYS ROWS OF TEETH AROUND ITS MOUTH AND A TONGUE THAT CAN SCRAPE AWAY SKIN AND SCALES.

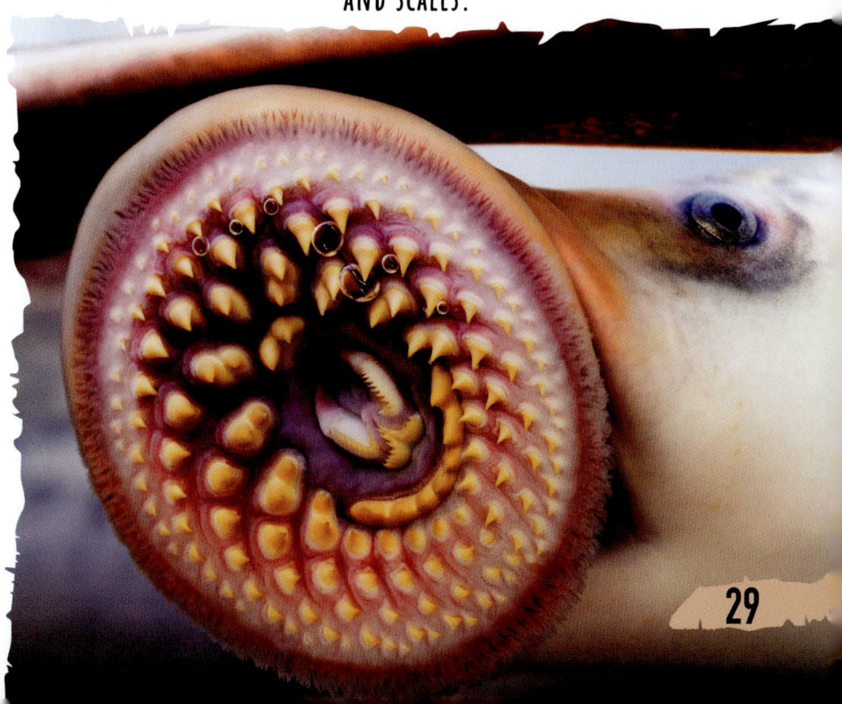

GLOSSARY

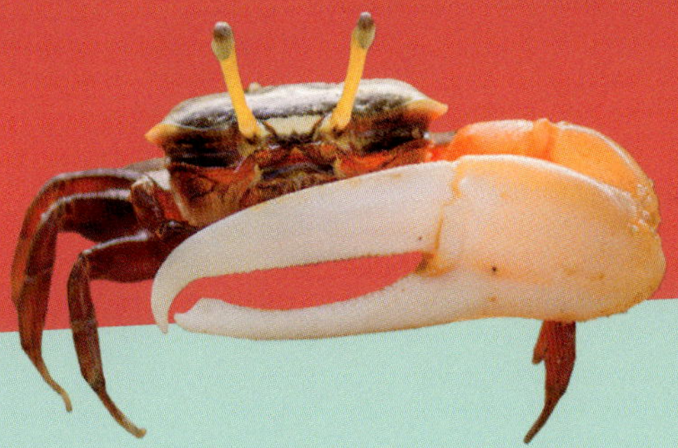

algae a simple aquatic plant, such as seaweed

canine tooth a sharp (often long) tooth

cartilage flexible tissue that forms the skeleton of some fish

cetacean a whale, dolphin, or porpoise

coral reef a hard ridge in the sea made of coral – a stony substance made from the skeletons of tiny sea animals

crevice a narrow opening or crack (in rock)

echolocation to locate objects using reflected sound

estuary the mouth of a river where the sea's tides flood in

exoskeleton hard cover of an invertebrate's body – especially spiders, insects, and crustaceans

gills organs that extract oxygen from water

food chain a series of plants and animals that depend on each other for food

habitat the natural home of a plant or animal

invasive species a non-native species that has been introduced to an area and that harms that environment

mammal a warm-blooded animal with a backbone, has hair or fur at some stage in its life, and is fed on its mother's milk when young

marine relating to the ocean

mucus slimy substance made by animals for either lubrication or protection

nocturnal active at night

predator an animal that hunts and kills other animals for food

prey an animal that is hunted for food (noun); to hunt and kill for food (verb)

reptile an animal with scaly skin, whose body temperature is the same as the environment around it. Reptiles may bask in the sun to warm up or seek shade to cool down

senses the five main senses are hearing, sight, smell, taste, and touch

serrated having a jagged edge

spawn to release or deposit eggs

subtropical relating to the areas just outside the tropics

territory an area defended by an animal against others of the same species

toxic something that is poisonous

tropical relating to the tropics, the areas of Earth just north and south of the equator

vertebrate an animal with a backbone; mammals, fish, and birds are all vertebrates

FURTHER INFORMATION

BOOKS

Great White Sharks vs. Dolphins by Ben Hubbard (Lerner Publications, 2025)

The Oceans Explored by Claudia Martin (Wayland, 2021)

The Big Picture: Oceans by Jon Richards (Franklin Watts, 2021)

WEBSITES

Check out the BBC bitesize website for lots of information relevant to this book and information on food chains.
www.bbc.co.uk/bitesize/topics/zx882hv/articles/z3c2xnb

National Geographic gives good introductions to the lifestyles of a range of fish. These are some of the best.

Anglerfish: www.kids.nationalgeographic.com/moment-of/article/moment-of-yikes
Bottlenose dolphin: www.natgeokids.com/uk/discover/animals/sea-life/dolphins/
Bull shark: www.kids.nationalgeographic.com/animals/fish/facts/bull-shark
Electric eel: www.kids.nationalgeographic.com/animals/fish/facts/electric-eel
Great white shark: www.kids.nationalgeographic.com/animals/fish/facts/great-white-shark
Green sea turtle: www.kids.nationalgeographic.com/animals/reptiles/facts/green-sea-turtle
Hammerhead shark: www.kids.nationalgeographic.com/animals/fish/facts/hammerhead-shark
Red-bellied piranha: www.kids.nationalgeographic.com/animals/fish/facts/red-bellied-piranha
Red lionfish: www.nationalgeographic.com/animals/fish/facts/red-lionfish
Stingray: www.kids.nationalgeographic.com/animals/fish/facts/stingray
Tiger shark: www.nationalgeographic.com/animals/fish/facts/tiger-shark

INDEX